I0625944

My Life

By Dr. Dorothy L. Pattrick

My Life

© 2025 Dr. Dorothy L. Pattrick
All rights reserved. This book or any portion thereof may not be reproduced in any form without permission from the copyright holder, except as permitted by U.S. Copyright Law.

Written By: Dr. Dorothy L. Pattrick
Cover Designed By: Aaron C. Butler
Edited By: Aaron C. Butler

Paperback ISBN: 9781967082223
eBook ISBN: 9781967082230
Library of Congress Control Number: 2025906042

Printed in the United States of America

BookButler Publishing Company
Upper Marlboro, MD 20774

TheBookButler.com

BookButler Publishing Company titles may be purchased in bulk for educational, business, fundraising, or sales promotional use. For information, please email: info@thebookbutler.com

Dedication

This book is dedicated to everyone who has faced hardship. Through my testimony, I hope My Life brings encouragement, strength, and healing to those in need. May it remind you to let go, trust God, and find peace in His plan. No matter what you've been through, know that deliverance is possible.

God bless you,
Dr. Dorothy L. Pattrick

Table of Content

Chapter 1

Aunt Susie's
Doll Baby

I was born on March 1, 1962, in Easton, Maryland, at Easton Memorial Hospital. From what I've been told, my birth was not easy—my mother almost died bringing me into this world. I never heard this from her directly, but I would catch bits and pieces when she testified about it in church. It wasn't until I was a teenager that I fully understood the danger she had been in. Maybe that should have made me feel closer to her, knowing how much she had gone through. But it didn't. From the moment I was born, our connection was fragile, distant, and unspoken.

I didn't stay with my mother after birth. Instead, I went home with Aunt Susie Green, the woman who became my whole world. She was a strong, loving woman with hands that worked tirelessly and a heart full of wisdom. She never had children of her own, but she had raised many of her nieces and nephews, and I was the last one. To me, she was everything. She was home.

Aunt Susie called me "Doll Baby" and spoiled me in ways I wouldn't fully appreciate until much later. She was a woman of routine—her house was always spotless, and she had a reputation in town for being the best at cleaning geese. People would bring their birds to her, and she'd pluck them clean, preparing them for cooking. She even taught me how to do it, and when she got paid, she made sure I got a share of the money. I loved the days we spent together in the kitchen, the smell of her famous chicken and mac and cheese filling the air. She grew her own fruits and vegetables and made the best jellies and apple butter I'd ever tasted. But more than anything, she gave me something I didn't even realize I was craving—hugs, warmth, and unconditional love.

I never felt like I was missing anything. I had a mother. Or at least, I thought I did. Then, one ordinary day when I was five, everything changed.

I don't remember when I first heard the name "Mary M. Brown," but I do remember the day I learned who she was. A strange man arrived at our house. His face was unfamiliar, his presence unsettling. I watched as Aunt Susie's expression shifted—something I couldn't quite understand at the time. Then, the words came.

"You have to go with him."

Go where? Why? My chest tightened. I didn't know this man. I didn't want to go anywhere. But before I could protest, I learned the first shocking truth—he was my grandfather. And then, the second—a name I had heard before but never thought much about suddenly carried the weight of a lifetime.

Mary M. Brown.

"She's your real mother," he said, "It's time for you to start school."

My mother? My real mother? No, that couldn't be right. Aunt Susie was my mother. She had always been my mother. The only mother I had ever known.

And yet, in that moment, everything I had believed, everything that had felt safe and true, collapsed around me.

I clung to Aunt Susie, sobbing, begging her not to make me go. She held me close and whispered that everything would be okay and that she would always be there for me. But I didn't want to go. I didn't want to leave the only home I had ever known.

When I arrived at my mother's house, nothing felt right. It wasn't home. It was cold and unfamiliar, and I felt like a stranger in my own family. Up until that moment, I had lived in the comfort of Aunt Susie's love, completely unaware that she wasn't my mother. The truth came crashing down on me all at once—I was not her daughter. And my real mother, the woman I had never known, was a stranger to me.

That first night in my mother's house, I lay in bed feeling lost, missing Aunt Susie's arms around me. The warmth, the safety, the sense of belonging—it was all gone. I didn't know then just how much my world had changed, but deep down, I knew that nothing would ever be the same again.

Chapter 2

The Weight of Unspoken Truths

Silence had always been a part of my life. Not the quiet that brings peace, but the kind that weighs heavy, pressing down like a secret no one dares to say out loud. In my family, we didn't talk about the hard things—pain, shame, and everything in between got tucked away beneath forced smiles and unfinished sentences.

I never knew the truth about my birth. Not at first. And when I finally learned it, it wasn't through a single conversation or a heartfelt confession. Instead, it came in bits and pieces—half-heard whispers and looks exchanged between adults who thought I wasn't paying attention. Even as a child, I knew when something was being hidden from me.

The man who fathered me wasn't just absent—he was a ghost I wasn't supposed to acknowledge. A man who had taken what he wanted, leaving my mother with a child she hadn't asked for and a wound that would never fully heal. He was older, married with kids, and a rapist.

My grandmother—the one person who should have protected both of us—made it clear that I was the consequence of something shameful. She wanted nothing to do with me. She was the one who had decided I didn't belong. And my mother… she just let it happen.

My mother now existed in my life, but only in the way a shadow exists—always there, but never warm, never real. She could talk to others, could laugh and love them, but with me, there was always a distance. I tried, again and again, to bridge that gap. I tried to make her see me. I tried to be good, to be enough. But no matter how hard I reached, she never reached back. I didn't understand it then, but looking back, I wonder if every time she saw me, she saw the man who violated her and left her with a permanent reminder. Maybe loving me meant facing that pain, and she just couldn't do it. I tried to make sense of it, but the pain of rejection still left its mark. It molded me in ways I wouldn't fully recognize until years later—hidden in the fractures of relationships I couldn't sustain, in the hesitation to let anyone in, in the marriages that crumbled under the weight of wounds I didn't have the words to explain.

The irony of it all was that the woman who truly raised me—Aunt Susie—wasn't even my mother. She was my great-aunt, my biological father's aunt. And yet, she was the only one who ever made me feel safe, the only real warmth I had ever known. From time to time, she would come to visit, and for those moments, the weight on my shoulders felt lighter. I could breathe. I wished I could stay with her forever, but life doesn't work that way.

Every time Aunt Susie left, my mother's resentment grew. Those were some of her meanest moments. But no matter how bad it got, I still held on, counting down the days until Aunt Susie's next visit. My mother's jealousy was obvious—I could see it in her eyes, hear it in her tone. I had always called Aunt Susie "Mom," but I quickly learned that if I wanted to keep the peace, I had to start calling her "Aunt Susie" whenever my mother was around.

I remember the first time I met my father. Aunt Susie had taken me to visit her sister—my grandmother on his side. I didn't know what to expect. I had spent so many years wondering about him, imagining what he might be like. And then there he was, standing right in front of me. I asked him—straight out—if he was my father. He just shrugged. No words, no acknowledgment, no nothing. It was as if I didn't exist. He had erased me before I even had the chance to know him.

That moment told me everything I needed to know.

Years passed, and the pain remained. But so did my search for understanding. As an adult, I see things differently. My mother and I were both black sheep, outcasts for things beyond our control. And while she never gave me the love I craved, I know now that her silence wasn't just about me. It was about her own wounds, ones she never had the chance to heal. If she were alive today, I would tell her that I understand—that I love her anyway.

Because sometimes, even without words, the truth still finds a way to be heard.

Chapter 3

Innocence Stolen

Summers at Bryan's United Methodist Church were supposed to be a time of fun, friendship, and freedom. I was seven or eight years old, eager to spend my days with "The Gang," a tight-knit group of girls I had grown close to—Judy, Dorothy, Jeanetta (who we called Faye), Karen, Julie, Betty, and Diane. We laughed together, played outside, and helped set up for meals, a role I especially loved because it reminded me of being at Aunt Susie's house. Serving others came naturally to me; even at that age, I found joy in it.

The summer program was new to me, but I quickly grew to love it. It was one of the few places where I felt a sense of belonging, even though I struggled with making friends at times. Church itself never really connected with me—outside of being forced to go with my grandmother—but the summer program was different. It was filled with games, playtime, and laughter. It felt safe. At least, it was supposed to be.

That day started like any other, with our group running around and probably laughing about something Faye said. Our world was small and innocent. Then, two men approached us—strangers we had never seen before. One of them pointed at me and told me to come with him. The other did the same to one of my friends. I don't remember which girl it was, but I remember how easily we obeyed.

We had been raised to listen to adults, to do as we were told without question. So, we followed.

The men led us to the church annex, a quiet building separate from where the other children played. Inside, they took us to a dark room—the boiler room. Then, he told me to take off my pants and lay down.

I didn't understand.

"What are we doing?" I asked.

He didn't answer.

I did what I was told, not because I understood, but because I had always been taught to obey. I heard my friend next to me crying, and then I felt it—pain so sharp it stole my breath. A terrible, gut-wrenching feeling that told me something was very wrong. But I was too young to know what. Too young to fight back. I just cried, too.

And then, just as quickly as it began, it was over. The men pulled up their pants and walked away as if nothing had happened—as if they hadn't just shattered something inside me that I didn't yet have words for.

I got dressed as fast as I could and left the annex with my friend. I don't remember if we spoke, if we looked at each other, or if we just ran back to the other children in silence. I just remember wanting to be anywhere but there.

As soon as I returned, I told one of the adults at the program what had happened. I don't know what I expected—comfort, safety, someone to make it all go away. But instead of protecting me, the adults failed me.

She told my mother. My mom said nothing to me about it.

16

When I got home, my grandmother was waiting for me, a switch in her hand.

"What did you do?" she asked, her voice sharp and accusing.

I didn't understand the question. I had done nothing.

"I don't know what it was," I told her, my voice small, my body still aching.

I thought she was going to whip me. Maybe, in some twisted way, that would have made more sense than the way she looked at me—as if I had brought this upon myself. But she never struck me. She just left me there, standing in the weight of my confusion and shame.

We never talked about it again.

The next day, I returned to the summer program as if nothing had happened. I forced myself to smile, to laugh with my friends, to act like everything was normal because normal was the only way I knew how to survive.

I saw the man again on the way there. I expected fear, maybe even anger. But I felt nothing—just emptiness. My mother confronted him — not with rage, not with the police, but with a warning. "If you ever touch my daughter again, I'll have you arrested," she told him. That was it: just a threat, just words. And then we walked away.

The only person who truly reacted was Aunt Susie. The weekend after it happened, I told her everything. Unlike my mother and grandmother, she was furious. She wanted justice. She wanted blood. She wanted to go get her gun and go after him.

For a moment, I thought she might actually do it.

But she didn't.

And so, I carried it.

I never spoke about it again. Not to my mother. Not to my grand-mother. Not even to my friend who had been there with me. We acted as if it had never happened because that was the only way to move forward.

But some things don't just go away.

Some things take pieces of you that you can never get back.

Chapter 4

A Lesson in Belonging

Some of my earliest memories of pride came from the classroom. I was a quiet child, always unsure of where I fit in at home, but at school, I had a place. In kindergarten, that place was at the top of the spelling bee. I loved words and loved the way letters fit together like tiny puzzle pieces, each one holding meaning. That day, I was the last student standing on my team, spelling word after word correctly while my classmates cheered me on.

When my teachers, Mrs. Pulley and Mrs. Green, told me to go to the principal's office and share the news with Mrs. Emory, I felt like I was floating. I had won. Me. The little girl who never felt seen at home had finally done something worth celebrating. Mrs. Emory smiled and told me she was proud of me, a rare moment where I felt truly valued.

But that feeling of accomplishment didn't last long.

At the end of first grade, despite doing well in my classes, I found myself in the same grade again the following year. I wasn't struggling, I wasn't failing—but still, I was made to stay behind. I don't know what my mother said to the principal or why she wanted me to repeat first grade, but I never questioned her. You dare not question my mother.

Watching my classmates move on to second grade without me stung in ways I couldn't put into words. Some of them I knew I was smarter than, yet there I was, sitting at a desk I had already outgrown. The new first-grade teacher barely had to teach me; I had already learned the material once before. It was an easy year academically, but inside, I felt something crack. Maybe my mother saw something wrong in me that I couldn't see. Maybe I really didn't belong.

By fourth grade, school had become a different kind of battlefield. My teacher, Aunt Phyllis, made it her mission to make my life miserable. She was my uncle's wife, someone I had known but never been close to. And in her classroom, I felt like I couldn't breathe.

She accused me of everything—talking back, skipping assignments, showing off. Even when I had done nothing wrong, I knew my name would be the first she called out. And at the end of each school day, she made sure my mother and grandmother knew exactly what kind of "trouble" I had caused. That meant daily punishments and whippings that left marks on my skin and my spirit. Some nights, I cried myself to sleep, wondering what I had done to deserve her hatred.

The only thing that gave me relief was knowing that one day, fourth grade would end. I made sure to keep my grades up so I could escape that classroom and the woman who seemed determined to break me.

By middle school, I had learned how to bury my anger. I stayed quiet and kept to myself. I begged my mother to let me move back in with Aunt Susie, the one place I had ever felt truly safe. When she finally said yes, I thought things would get better.

For a moment, they did.

Living with Aunt Susie was supposed to be my fresh start. But within a month of moving in, my cousin and her husband—two people who were supposed to be family—began violating me in ways I never could have imagined. Each of them, separately. Each of them, when we were alone. I don't even think they knew what the other was doing.

I stayed there for two years, trapped in silence. I never told Aunt Susie. I couldn't. I knew it would break her heart, and I couldn't bear to bring her that pain.

I started searching for love in all the wrong places. I didn't understand my worth, and I mistook attention for affection. That confusion led me into situations I never should have been in. I ended up having sex with someone I later found out was my brother on my father's side—something no one had ever told me. The realization shook me, but by then, the damage had already been done.

Not long after, I met a man and started spending time with him. Our relationship quickly became physical, and one day, a neighbor walked in on us having sex. Word spread fast. My aunt confronted me, asking if what she had heard was true. I couldn't bring myself to answer—I just stood there, silent, knowing there was no way to explain it in a way that would make sense to her.

Around the same time, I picked up smoking. One evening, my aunt's boyfriend caught me outside with a cigarette. Before he even said a word, I flicked it out and went inside, hoping he'd let it go. He didn't. He told my aunt, and once again, I found myself in trouble.

Through all of this, molestation from my cousin and her husband persisted. It felt like, more often, my cousin looked for opportunities to corner me alone to fondle my breasts and touch between my legs. Her husband was sneaking around making me go down him every chance he got. Juggling time between multiple men and sneaking off to smoke was becoming too much for me—especially at my age. Something had to change. I knew I couldn't stay at Aunt Susie's any longer. I didn't explain why; I just told her I had to go. We both cried. She wanted me to stay, and deep down, I wanted that too. But I left, making my way back to my mother's house once again.

Returning home was like stepping into a storm. My mother made sure I felt every bit of her resentment. By then, she was no longer living with my grandmother. Instead, she had moved in with her cousin. I never knew what caused the sudden change—our family didn't share much. And if they did, I was never included. I was always the outsider.

Life in our new home was different, not in a good way. My mother began treating me like a servant, expecting me to cook every meal and handle all the cleaning. The only time she seemed satisfied with me was when I was meeting her demands. It was a heavy burden for a middle schooler, especially as I struggled to keep up with my schoolwork. But no matter how much I tried or how much I longed for kindness, my needs and feelings never seemed to matter.

I didn't realize it then, but my life was on the verge of another shift—one that would take me down a road I wasn't ready for.

High school brought new challenges. The work was hard, but instead of offering help, my counselor placed me in special education classes. I wasn't slow, but sitting in those classrooms, labeled as something I wasn't, made me feel small. The teasing was relentless, and the isolation was worse.

I wanted so badly to belong that I made a desperate choice. I met a girl at school, someone I thought could be my friend. Instead of letting a friendship form naturally, I tried to buy it. I stole money from Aunt Susie and paid her to be my friend.

It worked—at least for a little while. But secrets never stay hidden forever.

The principal called me in one day, and when the weight of it all became too much, I confessed everything. I admitted that I had stolen the money and who I had given it to. Then, I faced the consequences.

Court was terrifying. My mother, my aunt, the girl, and her mother were all there. My lawyer stood beside me, but I still felt alone. The judge ruled that I had to pay the money back—me, not my mother.

Aunt Susie never stopped loving me. Even after everything, she forgave me. I must have apologized a hundred times, but she never held it against me.

Not long after that, Aunt Susie passed away.

I never thought our time together would be so short. She had heart issues, but I always assumed we had more time. I didn't just lose her—I lost my safe place, my protector, the one person who had always made me feel like I mattered.

I was left with a mother who didn't love me, a world that didn't make sense, and a desperate need to belong somewhere. Anywhere.

And so, I continued looking in all the wrong places.

Chapter 5

A Night of Awakening

Growing up, church was always a part of my life, but for a long time, it felt more like an obligation than a source of joy. My grandmother and mother made sure I was there every Sunday, and though I loved singing in the choir, the services often felt long and uneventful. My earliest memories of church were of Sunday school, where my kindergarten principal was the teacher. That familiarity made it comfortable, but as I got older, my interest wavered. If I wasn't singing, I was bored.

That started to change when I became more involved. Singing was my passion, and I wanted to be in the Young Adult Choir, even though they said I was too young. But I didn't let that stop me. I went to the preacher and asked him myself. He intervened, and soon, I was the youngest member of the choir, standing beside people much older than me, belting out songs I had grown up listening to. It was one of the happiest times in my young life. My family was known for their voices—the Brown family had a reputation for singing at churches all over town. We were even invited to be part of a church play, *Slab Town,* and though I only had two lines, I was thrilled to be on stage.

As I got older, my interest in church deepened beyond singing. I wanted to know more about God. My mother was a lay speaker, and I began attending Monday night classes with her, hoping it would be something we could bond over. But she never showed much interest. We rarely spoke about it. Still, I kept going, determined to find meaning in my faith.

One night, when I was in high school, something happened that changed everything.

That evening, my mother and I had gone to the family house, and she told me to stay inside. It was a school night, and she didn't want me going anywhere. But from the window, I saw the lights on at Robinson A.M.E. Church, and more importantly, I saw the cars— so many of them. Something was happening over there, something big. Curiosity got the best of me. I had to know what was going on.

As I approached the church, I could hear the music before I even stepped inside. The sound was electric. The congregation was alive in a way I had never seen before—people were singing, shouting, and crying out to God. The spirit was moving through the church like a rushing wind, and I felt something stir in me, something I couldn't explain.

I slipped inside quietly, trying to take it all in. My heart pounded. I wasn't just watching a service; I was experiencing something powerful. Then, the pastor spoke.

"If there's anyone here tonight who wants to be saved, come forward."

Before I could even think, my feet moved. I was walking toward the altar, my body acting before my mind caught up. My hands trembled, my chest felt light, and suddenly, a wave of emotion crashed over me. Tears welled in my eyes, but I wasn't sad. I was overwhelmed with joy and peace that something deeper than words could capture.

"I want to be saved," I whispered to the pastor.

He smiled, "Then tonight, you are saved."

Something inside me shifted at that moment. I knew I belonged to God.

When the service ended, I lingered, reluctant to leave. But I knew I had to get home before my mother noticed I was gone. As I slipped through the front door, I barely had time to brace myself before she hit me.

"Where have you been?" she demanded, her face tight with anger.

"I was at the revival at Robinson A.M.E.," I said, still feeling the warmth of what had just happened.

She scoffed, "Those people got you nervous! Go to bed."

Nervous? That wasn't what I felt. It was something special, something real. But I didn't argue. I went to bed, still buzzing with the feeling of God's presence.

A few days later, back at my aunt's house, something even stranger happened. I was alone in the living room, not praying, not listening to music, just sitting quietly when, suddenly, I was on the floor. I didn't know how I got there. My body felt different—light, yet full of energy, almost as if I was floating.

A neighbor came over and saw me. He knelt beside me, a knowing look on his face.

"You got the Holy Ghost," he said simply.

I stared at him, still trying to make sense of what had just happened. He didn't explain further, and at that moment, I was too caught up in the experience to ask questions. But I knew this wasn't random. This was something bigger than me.

After that night, I couldn't go back to the way things were. I still went to church with my mother, but I was different. My praise was louder. I clapped harder. I sang with a new kind of passion. When I felt the spirit, I didn't hold back—I shouted, I danced. But my mother's church wasn't like that. They didn't believe in outward expressions of praise.

"Sit down," they'd tell me when I got too excited.

But I just got back up.

Looking back, I know now that night at the revival was a turning point. It was the moment my faith became my own. It didn't matter that my mother dismissed it or that my church didn't understand it. God had called me, and I had answered.

Now, as a pastor, I make sure no one has to walk away from an experience like that feeling confused or alone. I explain, I guide, I encourage. Because I know what it's like to be young and on fire for God, yet surrounded by people who don't understand.

And I know that night, all those years ago, set me on the path to who I was always meant to be.

Chapter 6

When the
Party Ends

The day I moved out of my mother's house, I felt nothing but relief. There was no sadness, no second-guessing—just a sense of freedom I had never felt before. I had spent my childhood feeling like an outsider in my own home, like I was only there to cook, clean, and take care of my mother. There was no warmth, no real bond between us. So, when I graduated high school, I wasted no time making a plan. It took me about a month to find a job and a place to stay, and as soon as everything was in place, I told my mother I was leaving. She didn't say a word. She didn't ask where I was going, if I needed help, or even why I had made the decision. It was as if I had just told her I was going to the store.

That silence made my decision even easier.

For a month, we lived in the same house without speaking. On the day I moved, I packed up what little I had, got a ride to my new place in Easton, and never looked back.

My first place was in a two-story house, though I only lived on the first floor. I had a bedroom near the kitchen and bathroom, and I never had any reason to go upstairs. The house was always cold, but it didn't matter—I was free. I had roommates, but I mostly kept to myself when I was home. My real life was happening outside of those walls.

I worked at a seafood packing company, standing on an assembly line, boxing up frozen scallops, crab cakes, and fish to be sold in grocery stores. The job was repetitive, but I loved it. I made friends there, real friends. We ate lunch together, laughed, and made plans for the weekends. I finally felt like I belonged somewhere. And when Friday night came around, we hit the club.

Located just down the street from my house, the club was my escape. It was loud, full of life, and full of people who, like me, just wanted to forget about everything else. It wasn't just about drinking or dancing—it was about feeling free. For the first time, I had control over my life. No one was telling me what to do or how to act. I could just be me. I started helping out at the club, helping take orders on the bar side.

One night, my favorite song came on, and I turned to the nearest man and asked him to dance. He didn't hesitate. We danced and danced, never leaving the dance floor. Song after song played, and neither of us sat down. When a slow song came on, he pulled me close, and for the first time, I really looked at him.

His name was Wayne.

At the end of the night, Wayne asked me to sit with him, and we talked until the club closed at four in the morning. Before I left, he asked if he could walk me home. I let him. He waited as I helped clean up the bar area, and when we got to my door, he simply said goodbye—no hug, no kiss, just a quiet, respectful farewell.

I thought I had just made a new friend.

Over the next few weeks, Wayne kept coming back to the club, and we always found each other. We talked and laughed, and eventually, he invited me to visit him in St. Michaels for the weekend. I didn't see any harm in it. I loved meeting new people, and he had never given me a reason to be cautious.

At first, things were good. St. Michaels had its own little bar, and we would go there together, spending hours drinking and talking. After about six months, things shifted. Our conversations became deeper and more personal. We officially started dating, and before I knew it, I had moved in with him and his mother.

Two years into our relationship, I got pregnant.

I wasn't expecting it. One day at work, I suddenly felt over-heated. A friend took one look at me and said, "You're pregnant." I laughed it off, but something in the back of my mind nagged at me. I made a doctor's appointment, and sure enough, I got the call a few days later. "Congratulations," the doctor said. I was in shock.

That night, I met Wayne at the bar and told him. He didn't say much; just nodded and kept drinking. But the next morning, he told me I needed to get an abortion.

I refused.

He didn't push the issue again, but things between us started to unravel. One day, I came home and caught him having sex with an-other woman—one of my coworkers. I lost it. I attacked them both, my rage taking over, but then I remembered the life growing inside me. I forced myself to stop, to walk away. That night, I packed up my things and moved in with his aunt.

That's when I learned the full truth. Wayne wasn't just cheating on me—he had multiple women, and one of them was pregnant, too.

Despite everything, I had to live for the baby growing inside me. But life had one more twist in store for me.

An explosion at my job triggered premature labor. In the early hours of the morning, in the back of an ambulance, I gave birth to my son, Wayne Anthony Young Jr. He was due in December, but he arrived much earlier, fragile and small. Wayne showed up at the hospital later that morning, but he wasn't the man I needed him to be.

The early days of motherhood were some of the hardest times of my life. Because my son was born prematurely, he had to be transferred to Francis Scott Key Hospital to receive better care. It broke my heart to leave him there, but I knew it was the best place for him. During that time, I moved out of Wayne's aunt's house and got a two-bedroom duplex for just the two of us. I wanted to create a stable home for my baby, even though I was figuring everything out on my own.

Wayne was put on child support, but he didn't want to pay it. Instead, he offered to move in with me so we could raise our son together. I agreed, and I took him off child support, thinking maybe things would be different this time.

Wayne had always been a drinker, but he was now drinking much more often. He was also using drugs, disappearing for days at a time. At first, I ignored the signs. I didn't want to believe the whispers, the warnings from women who had been in my shoes before. But one night, everything changed.

I had gone out with my friends to the club, something Wayne hated. He wanted to keep me away from there because that's where he met other women. That night, he lost control. In front of everyone, he dumped his drink on my head, humiliating me. A bartender stepped in, and before I knew it, Wayne was in a fight. He didn't stop there. He was inappropriate with a woman at the bar and when her boyfriend stepped in. Wayne picked a fight with him. This man had a gun. A shot rang out, people screamed, and the night ended with Wayne in the back of an ambulance, beaten and bloodied.

It should have been my wake-up call, but it wasn't.

The abuse didn't start all at once. It was little things—jealousy, possessiveness, controlling behavior. Then, the physical violence began. A slap here, a shove there. I told myself it wasn't that bad. I told myself he would change.

But he didn't.

One night, I was upstairs and decided to go down to the kitchen to warm up some food because I was hungry. While I waited, I went to sit in the living room and noticed Wayne on the couch, partially dressed, pretending to watch TV. Something felt off. Then, I saw the closet door—it was cracked open when I knew for a fact I had closed it. My heart started racing as I walked over and pulled the door open. There she was—the same woman Wayne had cheated on me with before—hiding in my closet, also half-dressed.

I saw red. I attacked her and threw her out of my house. I was done. I told Wayne he needed to leave, and the next morning, he was gone.

But he didn't stay away for long. He kept coming back, wanting to spend time with me, trying to stay over. I was tired of living this way—tired of the back and forth, tired of doing things that I knew weren't right. I told him if he wanted to be in my life, we needed to get married. This wasn't the life I wanted, and it wasn't what God wanted for me, either.

Wayne agreed, and we got married quickly. Around that same time, after five long months in the hospital, Little Wayne was finally able to come home. Motherhood had already tested me in so many ways, but through it all, I was determined to fight for a better life for me and my son. Maybe it was because I was scared of raising a child alone. Maybe it was because I had spent so much of my life searching for a family, and I thought I had finally found one. Whatever the reason, I committed to being his wife and a mother to our son.

Life wasn't better. It was hell. For ten years, Wayne hurt me. Over and over again. And for ten years, I stayed.

Until one day, I didn't.

Wayne had been drinking, and I was walking down the street when he decided to attack me. A couple saw what was happening and called the police. We ended up in court, and for the first time, I saw things clearly.

This wasn't love.

I left.

But my escape came at a cost.

And that was a pain I wasn't sure I could survive.

Chapter 7

A Mother's Battle

Leaving my husband was only the beginning of the struggle. I had no support, no help, and no one to lean on. I was with my son twenty-four hours a day, seven days a week, with no break and no time to breathe. The weight of it all sat heavily on my shoulders. I tried to reach out for help—I pleaded with my husband, begged his mother, and even asked his sister to watch my son for just an hour or two so I could get some rest. But no one would help me. Not even for a moment.

I knew something was off inside me, but I didn't have the words to explain it. My emotions were out of control, and I found myself growing more and more frustrated. My patience wore thin. Some days, when my son cried and nothing I did could soothe him, I would shake him or pinch him out of sheer exhaustion and desperation. The realization of what I was doing terrified me. This wasn't who I was, but something was brewing inside me that I couldn't control. It felt like the weight of my entire life was crushing me, suffocating me, and I had no way to escape.

I stopped going to church. I stopped going to the bar. I stopped opening up to my friends because I didn't know how to explain what I was feeling. I was drowning, and no one even noticed.

Finally, I decided to seek help. I went to Social Services to see if they had any programs to assist struggling mothers like me. But they had nothing to offer. I left feeling even more defeated. Then, I decided to see a counselor. I didn't hold anything back during those sessions—I told her everything. The good, the bad, the things I never thought I'd say out loud. I confessed that I sometimes turned my anger onto my son, and for the first time in a long time, I felt a flicker of hope. Maybe, just maybe, things would get better.

A few days later, I was sitting in my apartment. My son was in his little chair, quiet for once, and the house felt peaceful. Then, a knock at the door shattered that peace. I opened it to find a woman standing there—a white woman who looked familiar. She was the same woman I spoke with when I visited Social Services to inquire about programs to help me. I knew why she was there. I didn't fight. I didn't argue. I just stood there, watching as she took my baby from my arms. The door closed, and I crumpled to the floor, crying harder than I ever had before.

My husband found out that our son had been taken, and instead of standing by me, he used it against me. He was angry and saw it as another reason to do whatever he wanted, as if he needed one. He continued seeing my ex-coworker, and soon, she became pregnant. That was the final blow. I couldn't take it anymore. We fought—physically, verbally, emotionally. I even fought her. I had lost control of my life, and I knew I needed to get away from him before I lost myself completely.

I called a local shelter and told them I needed to leave. They picked me up immediately, and I was grateful, but I hated being there. Each morning, we had to leave at a certain time, and we weren't allowed back in until the evening. There were no exceptions. It didn't matter if you had nowhere to go; you had to find something to do until it was time to return.

While I was in the shelter, I spent every moment fighting to get my son back. Court dates, meetings with caseworkers, endless paperwork—I did everything they asked. But it wasn't enough. The court decided my son would stay in foster care while I got my life together. At first, he was placed with my husband's mother, and even though she was supposed to keep him away from me, she secretly arranged visits. She believed a child should be able to see his mother.

But when Social Services asked if I had been seeing him, I told the truth. And just like that, he was taken from her and placed with strangers. That was my biggest mistake—I trusted the system. And the system failed me.

He was moved from one foster home to another. The first home was abusive. The second was with a woman who spoke badly about me to anyone who would listen. She even poisoned my son against me, feeding him lies about who I was. I went straight to Social Services and told them if they didn't handle it, I would take her to court myself. They looked into it, and things got better after that.

Through it all, I never stopped fighting for my son. Even when it became clear that I would never get him back, I refused to disappear from his life. I stayed in touch, visiting whenever I could. When he got older, we spoke on the phone every Saturday morning without fail. The only time we didn't talk was the one Saturday a month we visited each other. Even today, we see each other once a month— usually on a Saturday.

As I moved toward finalizing my divorce, I turned inward, focusing on my mental health for the first time in years. I needed to untangle the mess of emotions I had buried just to get through each day. In that process, I made amends with my ex-coworker, who now had a baby girl. I finally saw the truth: she wasn't my enemy. Like me, she had been caught in Wayne's web of empty promises and lies.

Looking back, I realize now that I was battling depression and anxiety, though I didn't have the words for it at the time. I just knew

I was struggling to survive. If I could tell my younger self anything, it would be this: *give yourself grace.* You didn't know then what you know now. You were fighting battles no one prepared you for. And while I thought I was finding my way to something better, I had no idea there was another storm coming.

Chapter 8

Breaking the Cycle

After my divorce, I tried to move forward. I wanted to believe that life would be better, that I would be wiser in love, and that the worst was behind me. But as I would come to learn, making the same choices leads to the same pain, and my next relationship would only prove that.

His name was Cecil. We met while working at a restaurant—he was a cook, and I was a waitress. At first, he was just a coworker, someone I saw during my shift and talked to as we closed up for the night. But over time, he made his intentions clear. He pursued me relentlessly. Every shift, he found a reason to linger, offering to help me with my side work, asking about my day, complimenting my hair or my smile. At first, I brushed it off. I knew he was living with another woman. I told myself I wasn't interested.

But Cecil had a way of wearing me down. He had charm, the kind that made you forget his faults if you weren't careful. He begged me to give him a chance, to let him come over, to see where things could go. I told myself I was strong enough to keep it casual, but deep down, I knew better. The truth was, I was lonely. I was still hurting from everything that had happened with Wayne, and Cecil knew just the right words to say.

For years, we were on and off. I was never the only woman in his life, but I convinced myself that maybe one day, I would be the last one standing. Eventually, he started spending more and more time at my place, until one day, he just never left. He was mine now—or so I thought.

It didn't take long for the same old patterns to resurface. People told me he was cheating, and I already knew. There were nights he didn't come home, excuses that didn't add up, whispers I tried to ignore. But the moment that broke me was the night I went looking for him.

He hadn't come home, and I had a feeling I knew where he was. I sat at the table with a knife in front of me, waiting, my anger boiling over. But when the sun started to rise, and he still wasn't home, I couldn't sit still any longer. I left the knife behind—thank God I did—and went to find him.

I knocked on the door of a woman I knew he had been seeing. When she opened it, I saw him standing behind her. He had no shame, no guilt, no hesitation. And somehow, instead of being furious, I felt empty. I had spent years hoping he would change, only to end up right back where I started—being made a fool of by a man who never really loved me.

That morning, I knew I couldn't do this anymore. I called one of the evangelists from my church, desperate for help, for someone to tell me how to make this pain stop. She prayed with me, calmed me down, and offered me a place to stay. Without hesitation, I packed my things and left.

For six months, I lived with the evangelist, finding comfort in her prayers and support. But eventually, I needed to stand on my own two feet again, so I moved into a shelter while I saved for my own place. When I finally got an apartment at Bradford House, I told myself I was done with Cecil.

But of course, he came back.

At first, it was just visits. Then, the visits got longer. Then, one day, he asked to stay. I should have said no. I should have remembered all the nights I cried over him, all the times he had made me feel like nothing. But I told myself it would be different. And just like I had done before, I convinced myself that marriage would fix things.

We got married at the courthouse, and for a moment, I was happy. I let myself believe that being his wife would make him love me the way I had always wanted him to.

But nothing changed.

Cecil still disappeared for nights at a time. He still lied. He still cheated. And worst of all, he didn't even bother to hide it. One night, I found out the other woman was someone I had known for years—someone I had confided in, laughed with, trusted. When I realized the betrayal, something inside me broke. It was Wayne all over again. It was my ex-coworker all over again. It was the same story, just a different name.

For ten years, I lived this cycle of heartbreak and false hope—ten years of lies, of infidelity, of emotional wounds that never had the chance to heal.

Then, one day, Cecil told me he was moving to Perrysville. He said he wanted a fresh start for both of us, that he was going back to school and finding a job. He said he had found a townhouse for us, a place where we could finally build a better life.

I wanted so badly to believe him.

I packed up my things and moved with him, telling myself that maybe this was the change we needed. Maybe, after a decade, he was ready to be the man I had always hoped he would be.

But it didn't take long for the truth to come out.

Cecil hadn't changed. He had just found a new woman in a new town.

I had been in Perrysville for less than three months when I realized I was sharing a home with Cecil and his demons. The cheating, the lies, the empty promises—it was all still there.

I couldn't do it anymore.

I packed my things and left, returning to Cambridge. This time, I didn't look back. I filed for divorce, knowing in my heart that there was nothing left to save.

Looking back now, I realize that what I thought was love was never love at all. It was longing. It was loneliness. It was the desperate hope that someone—anyone—would choose me.

If I could go back and tell my younger self anything, it would be this: never marry someone who isn't equally yoked. A relationship built on broken foundations will always collapse. And no matter how much you love someone, you can't make them love you the way you deserve.

Chapter 9

Letting Go and Letting God

In the years that followed, my faith deepened. I threw myself into ministry, immersing myself in both spiritual and academic growth. I had made a promise to myself—to be better, to do better, to heal from my past, and to walk fully in the purpose that God had placed on my life. But healing wasn't immediate, and it wasn't easy. It came in layers, in steps both forward and backward, through moments of clarity and moments of deep doubt.

I started counseling on September 22, 2005, during my marriage to Cecil. For three months, I sat in a chair, unburdening myself to a professional, peeling back the layers of pain, disappointment, and questions that had lived inside me for so long. At first, I questioned whether it would help. But I quickly realized that counseling was not about being "crazy" or weak—it was about choosing to heal. And for me, healing came from both therapy and spiritual counseling. I trusted God with my heart, but I also allowed myself the space to talk, to process, to release. It was the combination of both that kept me going.

Between 2005 and 2009, I focused on being a better person. I poured into my marriage, into my spiritual journey, and into my purpose. I knew God had called me to do more than exist—I was meant to serve. In 2009, I took a step that would change my life forever: I enrolled at the Christian World College of Theology.

It wasn't easy balancing my studies with everything else. There were moments of exhaustion, moments where I questioned if I could really do it. But I pressed forward, knowing that God had led me to this place. Although my marriage ended in 2010, the year was full of promise. In July, I received my Certificate of Bible Studies. A year later, in July 2011, I earned my Associate of Ministry. Each milestone was more than just a degree—it was a symbol of everything I had overcome. The nights of self-doubt, the weight of my past, the wounds that still lingered—they didn't hold me back. I kept going.

By May 2014, I stood in my cap and gown, receiving my Bachelor of Divinity from Eastern Shore School of Ministry. As I looked out into the audience, my heart swelled with emotion. I had invited my mother to the ceremony, but I hadn't expected her to come. She had never been one for celebrations, at least not where I was concerned. But there she was.

When the ceremony ended, I walked up to her and wrapped my arms around her. I was overjoyed, my heart full. I finally felt like she was proud of me. But just like every hug before, she didn't hug me back.

That moment should have broken me, but it didn't. I had learned that love, real love, isn't always about what you receive in return. It's about what you choose to give, even when it's not reciprocated. And despite everything, I was determined to honor my mother while she was alive to see it.

One year, I threw her a birthday party. For a brief moment, she was happy. But just as quickly as the joy appeared, it faded. The following year, I organized a birthday celebration service for her at her church and even preached at the event. Again, she seemed happy, but the warmth never lasted. Still, I kept trying. I kept reaching. I kept hoping.

But eventually, I had to let go.

I decided I would call her on Mondays, Wednesdays, and Fridays. No more than five minutes—just enough to check in but not enough to invite pain. I did it because I loved her. Because I hoped, one day, she would love me back.

Years passed, and I continued to pursue my education. In 2015, I received my Master's in Theology. And by 2017, I had completed my Doctorate in Divinity. Looking back, I knew none of it had been easy. But every late night, every tear, every sacrifice was worth it. I had not only defied the odds—I had proven to myself that I was capable of more than my past had dictated.

And then, something happened that I never expected.

In March 2020, I invited my mom to my birthday celebration at my church. And she came.

At that time, she was living in a nursing home. I started visiting her every other Saturday, not expecting much but simply wanting to be there. Slowly, something changed.

For the first time in my life, my mother began showing affection. She laughed with me. She joked. She reached out to me. She asked me to wash her hair, and when I did, I saw something in her eyes— appreciation.

She even started hugging me first.

I didn't need an apology. I didn't need explanations for the past. All I wanted was to hold onto these moments, to enjoy what we had now. And for the first time, I felt like I had a mother.

But time has a way of reminding us how fleeting it really is.

On the morning of September 26, 2020, I received a call from the nursing home.

"You need to come right away," they told me.

I made my way there as fast as I could, my heart pounding in my chest. When I arrived, my mother was in and out of consciousness. I sat beside her, holding her hand, praying over her. I told her it was okay—that she could rest—that she could go in God's arms.

And then, I had to do the hardest thing I had ever done.

I had to let her go.

She passed a short time after I left the nursing home.

I had spent my entire life longing for her love, fighting for it, aching for it. And in the end, I realized something—love doesn't always look the way we expect it to.

Sometimes, it comes in small moments, in unexpected gestures, in the quiet shifts that we never see coming. My mother may not have always shown love in the way I wanted, but in those final years, I believe she did love me.

And that was enough.

Letting go isn't about forgetting. It's about releasing the pain while holding onto the good. It's about moving forward with grace.

And as I continue my journey, I choose to walk in that grace. To keep loving. To keep serving. To keep letting God heal the broken places.

Chapter 10

Walking in My Purpose

My journey has been one of trials and triumphs, pain and healing, darkness and light. Through every challenge, I have come to understand that God has been my anchor, carrying me when I could not carry myself. The scars of my past still linger, but they no longer define me. Instead, they remind me of the strength I have found in God's love and the purpose He has placed upon my life.

I have spent years seeking healing from wounds that seemed impossible to mend. The longing for my mother's love is still there, but I have learned to rest in the assurance that God's love is more than enough. That understanding has given me peace, allowing me to let go of what I cannot change and embrace the blessings that are before me.

Even as I embrace the blessings of today, I continue to build toward the vision God has given me. My heart is deeply rooted in ministry, and I know that my purpose is to serve, teach, and uplift others. My war room—a sacred space in my home where I pray and seek God—has become my sanctuary. It is there that I pour out my worries, surrender my fears, and receive divine direction. Every dream I hold and every vision I pursue has been laid before God in that room, and I trust that He will continue to guide my steps.

A Vision for Ministry

God has placed a mighty calling on my life, and I refuse to sit on the gifts He has given me. My vision is to create a ministry that is more than just a church—it will be a movement, a haven, and a source of transformation for those in need.

At the heart of this vision is God's Way Outreach Center, a place where lives will be restored, hope will be renewed, and faith will be strengthened. This outreach center will serve as a refuge for the homeless, the elderly, troubled children, pregnant teens, and individuals struggling with addiction. It will be a place of healing, not just spiritually, but physically, mentally, and emotionally.

I envision multiple ministries operating within God's Way Outreach Center. There will be counseling services for those battling depression, addiction, and trauma. A Visiting Angels program will provide care and companionship for the elderly in their homes. A program called SWAG (Serving With A Giving Heart) will offer support for pet owners who struggle to care for their dogs while managing personal hardships.

For education, I plan to provide GED classes for those who never had the chance to complete school, as well as college scholarships and financial assistance for housing and essential needs. I want to ensure that every person, regardless of their circumstances, has the resources to build a better future.

A Christian Bookstore and Bible College

Beyond the outreach center, my heart burns for education and spiritual growth. I want to open a Christian bookstore where people can find Bibles, devotionals, and inspirational literature to nourish their souls. Alongside that, I dream of establishing a Bible College—a fully accredited institution that offers theological training, pastoral studies, and ministry leadership courses. My goal is to provide financial aid options so that anyone, regardless of their financial situation, can receive a biblical education.

This Bible College will not just be a place of learning—it will be a place of transformation. It will train leaders who are equipped to spread the Gospel, serve their communities, and walk boldly in their callings.

A Home for the Broken

Another part of my vision is to open transitional homes for those in need. These homes will serve:

- Women, teenage girls, and children who are escaping abusive environments or homelessness.

- Men and boys who need guidance, mentorship, and a fresh start.

These homes will not just provide shelter; they will offer counseling, life skills training, and spiritual mentorship to help residents transition into stable, independent lives.

A Call to Evangelism and Service

My life is dedicated to bringing souls to Christ—not just within the walls of a church but in the streets, communities, and wherever God sends me. I want to reach the lost, encourage the broken, and remind the forgotten that they are loved.

I see myself traveling, spreading the Gospel, hosting conferences and workshops, and being a motivational speaker who uplifts those who feel like they have no hope. My ministry is not meant to look like anyone else's—it is unique because my calling is unique.

I desire to live debt-free, own my businesses, and be financially stable—not for my own comfort, but so that I can pour back into the lives of others. I want to be a resource for those who need help, whether it's financial, emotional, or spiritual.

Walking in Obedience

Through all of this, my ultimate goal is to walk in obedience to God. I want to be the woman He has called me to be—to live, pray, preach, teach, and lead with integrity. Every dream I have is rooted in my desire to follow His voice and do what is right in His sight.

I have learned that obedience brings blessings, and when I surrender my plans to God, He takes them and multiplies them in ways I never could have imagined.

Letting Go of the Past, Embracing the Future

While my past has shaped me, it does not define me. I no longer dwell on what I have lost—I focus on what I have gained in Christ. The pain, the struggles, and the moments of feeling unloved have all been part of my refining process.

God has placed new people, new opportunities, and new purpose in my life, and I embrace them with an open heart. He has shown me that His love is greater than any human love I could ever long for, and in that truth, I find my peace.

As I continue to walk this journey, I know that challenges will come, but I face them with the confidence that I am not alone. God is with me, guiding my every step, and as long as I follow Him, I know that my future is secure.

This is only the beginning. My vision is unfolding, my purpose is being revealed, and I am ready to step boldly into the destiny that God has prepared for me.

I will serve. I will teach. I will lead.

And most importantly—I will continue to trust God, every step of the way.

The Journey Continues

My story is one of resilience, faith, and transformation. I have faced rejection, abuse, and loss, yet I stand firm in my belief that every trial has led me closer to God. My mission is clear: to uplift, to serve, and to spread the message of love and redemption.

To anyone reading this, know that your past does not define you. With faith, perseverance, and trust in God, you can overcome anything. I am living proof of that.

Philippians 4:13 – "I can do all things through Christ who strengthens me."

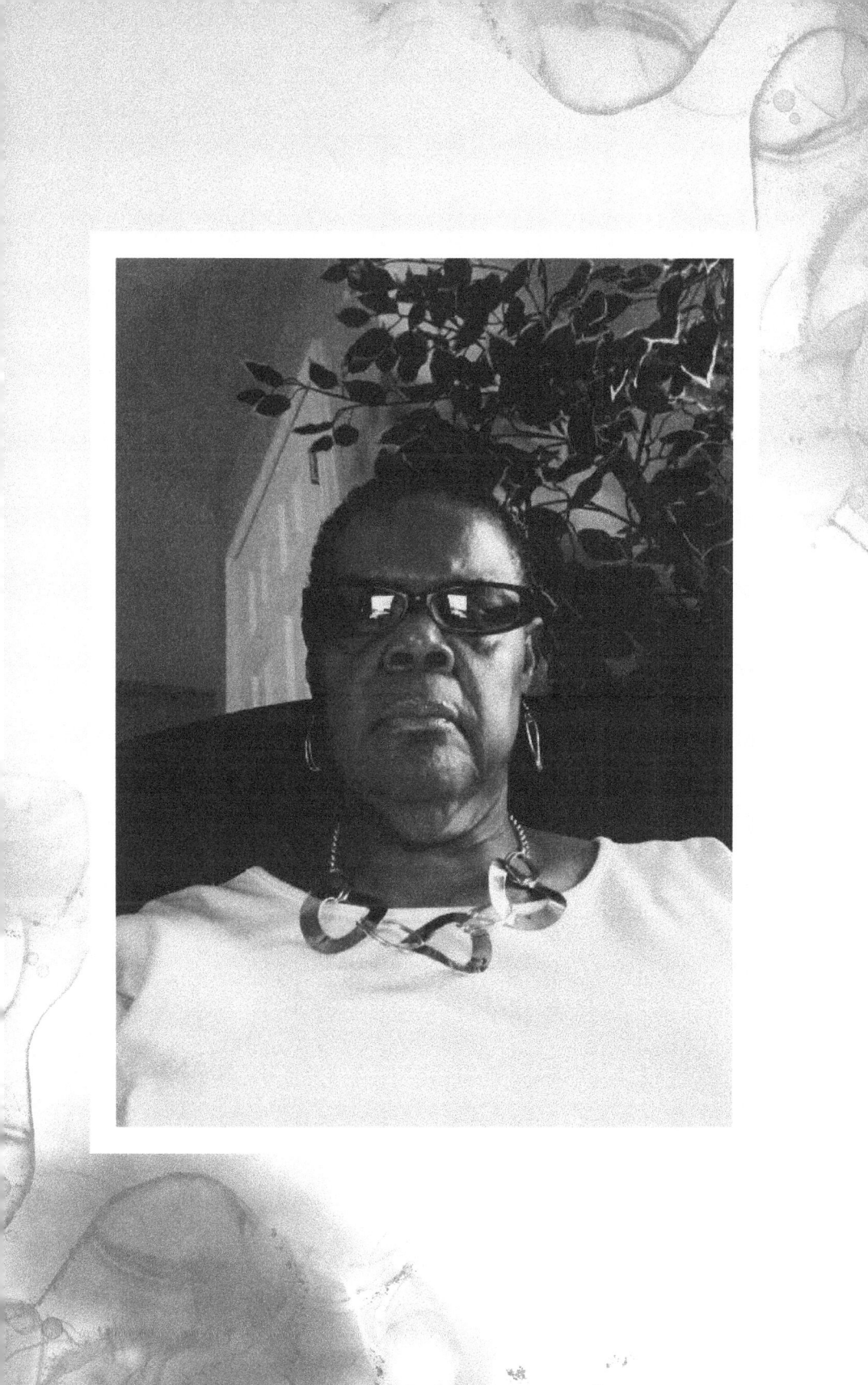

Little Wayne

About the Author

Dr. Dorothy L. Pattrick is a devoted minister, author, and speaker with a deep passion for God and His word. She gave her life to Christ in the 1970s at Robinson AME Church and grew in faith under the leadership of Apostle John Cornish Sr., Apostle Arlinda Cornish-Barnes, and the late Apostle Terry Dixon. She holds a Doctor of Divinity, a Master's in Theology, and multiple ministry certifications. Dr. Pattrick is the author of My Life, with additional books in progress. Beyond ministry, she loves traveling and embracing new challenges.

www.ingramcontent.com/pod-product-compliance
Lightning Source LLC
Chambersburg PA
CBHW051244120626
46547CB00014B/1784